SCHOLASTIC

Shoe Box Learning Centers

Alphabet

by Jacqueline Clarke

NEW YORK • TORONTO • LONDON • AUCKLAND • SYDNEY
MEXICO CITY • NEW DELHI • HONG KONG • BUENOS AIRES

Teaching Resources

Edited by Joan Novelli
Cover design by Maria Lilja
Cover photograph by James Levin/Studio 10
Interior design by Holly Grundon
Interior illustrations by James Graham Hale and Maxie Chambliss

ISBN 0-439-53792-4

Copyright © 2006 by Jacqueline Clarke.
Published by Scholastic Inc.
All rights reserved.
Printed in the U.S.A.
4 5 6 7 8 9 10   40   13 12 11 10 09 08

CONTENTS

About This Book

A B C D E F G . . . Alphabet recognition is essential to learning to read and write. As children learn to identify letters in and out of sequence and the sounds they represent, they build a foundation for understanding sound-spelling relationships. Providing plenty of practice in alphabet recognition helps build accuracy and speed, both of which make it easier for children to learn to read.

Shoe Box Learning Centers: Alphabet makes it easy to create 30 engaging, portable centers that help children learn the alphabet through hands-on exploration of letter names, their shapes, and their sounds. Each center fits neatly inside a shoe box and can be pulled out as needed and stored conveniently when not in use. Most shoe box activities are open-ended, which allows children to repeat the activity several times during center time, reinforcing skills all the while.

The book is organized into three sections: letter recognition, letter formation, and letter sounds. These centers will help children acquire the alphabetic knowledge needed to form the basic foundation for phonological awareness. Each center includes:

- **Label and Directions:** The title on the page becomes the box label. Simply glue it to one end of the shoe box for easy storage and retrieval. Cut out the student directions and glue them to the inside lid of the box.

- **Materials:** Check here to find out which items you'll need for each center. Most materials are inexpensive and readily available in your home or classroom.

- **Shoe Box Setup:** Here you'll find simple directions to assemble each center. In most cases, all you'll need to do is gather materials and make copies of reproducible pages.

- **Reproducible Pages:** Game boards, playful patterns, and record sheets are just some of the reproducibles included in this book. Laminate games and patterns, or copy them onto card stock for durability.

- **Tips:** Look here for helpful hints and extension activities.

Setting Up Shoe Box Learning Centers

The games and activities in *Shoe Box Learning Centers: Alphabet* are designed to be used by small groups of two to six students at centers but can easily be adapted for whole-class lessons, one-on-one teaching, or independent use. Use them to supplement your current literacy program and to spiral letter practice throughout the entire school year. Since many of the centers are adaptable for use with any letter, you can use them to reinforce your "letter of the week" as well as previously introduced letters.

Each center provides children with a concrete way to practice letter concepts using appealing hands-on manipulatives, such as letter cards, alphabet boards, picture cards, sound boards, finger-spelling cards, toy animals, alphabet "beans," even marshmallows and pasta!

To assemble the centers, photocopy each page on colored paper (or have children decorate), and cut out the title and directions along the lines as indicated. Glue the title to the outside of the box (on the end or side that will show when you stack and store the shoe boxes), and glue the student directions to the inside of the lid. Assemble and prepare any other necessary materials (such as the reproducible activity pages) and place these in the box. You may want to enlist parent volunteers or students to assist with this process.

To help students get the most out of using the centers, model the activities before inviting children to do them on their own.

Assessing Student Learning

Use the shoe box centers in this book to assess children's knowledge of the alphabet. The first ten centers provide opportunities to assess letter recognition. For example, with Breakfast Words (page 9), which letters are children able to correctly match to the names on the cereal boxes? Are there any letters that are confusing (for example *m* and *n* or *b* and *d*)? When children work with uppercase and lowercase letters, such as with Spill the Letters Match-Up (page 13), are they able to match and name them? The next set of centers offers opportunities to assess letter formation. Use these centers to observe children's understanding of the features of letters. For example, Alphabet Soup (page 40) invites them to explore curved and straight lines. The remaining set of centers reinforces letter sounds. The Sound Bus (page 62) lets you assess children's understanding of the letters that represent beginning, ending, and medial sounds in words. For all centers, the checklist on page 7 makes it easy to maintain brief anecdotal records of children's progress.

For activities that do not require the use of record sheets, sticky notes work well as an assessment tool. Observe and talk with students as they work with a shoe box center. Jot comments on sticky notes, and record the child's name, the date, and the shoe box center name. Store these notes on a separate sheet of paper in a pocket folder. In addition, comments for any center can be recorded on the checklist. Use these assessments to guide students' work at the centers. Encourage students to revisit those centers where they show a need for more practice.

Meeting the Standards for Language Arts

Mid-continent Research for Education and Learning (McREL), a nationally recognized nonprofit organization, has compiled and evaluated national and state standards—and proposed what Pre-K–12 teachers should provide for their students to grow proficient in language arts, among other curriculum areas. The centers in this book support students in meeting the following McREL benchmarks for Standard 5 (Uses the general skills and strategies of the reading process):

- recognizes that print and written symbols convey meaning and represent spoken language

- understands differences between letters, numbers, and words and knows the significance of spaces between words

- recognizes that print is read from left to right and top to bottom

- recognizes letters of the alphabet

- recognizes familiar words in print

- recognizes that print appears in different forms and serves different purposes

- recognizes familiar print in their environment

- uses basic elements of phonetic analysis (for example, common letter-sound relationships, beginning and ending consonants, vowel sounds, blends, word patterns) to decode unknown words

Source: *A Compendium of Standards and Benchmarks for Pre-K–12 Education* (Mid-continent Regional Educational Laboratory, 2004).

To match specific skills and shoe box centers, see the chart on page 8.

Shoe Box Learning Centers Checklist

Name_____

Shoe Box Learning Center	Date	Comments
Breakfast Words		
Spill the Letters Match-Up		
Conversation-Heart Messages		
Feely-Box Letters		
Up and Down the Beanstalk		
ABC Caterpillar		
The Mystery of the Missing Letters		
Lost and Found		
Match the Mix-Ups		
Trace and Race		
Letter Collages		
Snowy Day Letters		
Airplane ABCs		
Tweet-Tweet Letter Treats		
Rainy Day Writing		
Cups of Cocoa		
ABC Snapshots		
Alphabet Soup		
Cloudy Day ABCs		
Handmade Names		
Vroom! Vroom!		
B Is for Butterfly		
On Alphabet Street		
Buried Treasure		
It's a Parade!		
Check It Out!		
Musical Letters		
The Sound Bus		
Apples on a Tree		
All About My Name		

Meeting the Language Arts Standards

Shoe Box Learning Center	Uppercase Letters	Lowercase Letters	Uppercase and Lowercase Match	Letter Shapes	Letter/Sound Relationships	Alphabetical Order	Letter Formation	Word Parts	Beginning/Middle/Ending Sounds	Concepts of Print
Breakfast Words	X	X	X	X						X
Spill the Letters Match-Up	X	X	X	X						
Conversation-Heart Messages	X	X	X	X						X
Feely-Box Letters	X	X		X						
Up and Down the Beanstalk	X	X	X	X		X				
ABC Caterpillar	X	X	X	X		X				
The Mystery of the Missing Letters	X	X	X	X		X				
Lost and Found	X	X	X	X		X				
Match the Mix-Ups	X	X	X	X						
Trace and Race	X	X		X						
Letter Collages	X	X		X	X					
Snowy Day Letters	X	X		X	X		X			
Airplane ABCs	X	X		X	X		X			
Tweet-Tweet Letter Treats	X	X		X	X		X			
Rainy Day Writing	X	X		X	X		X			
Cups of Cocoa	X	X		X	X		X			
ABC Snapshots	X	X		X	X		X			
Alphabet Soup	X	X		X	X		X			
Cloudy Day ABCs	X	X		X	X		X			
Handmade Names	X	X			X		X			
Vroom! Vroom!	X	X		X	X					X
B Is for Butterfly	X	X		X	X					X
On Alphabet Street	X	X			X				X	
Buried Treasure	X	X		X	X	X			X	
It's a Parade!	X	X			X				X	
Check It Out!	X	X			X				X	
Musical Letters	X	X		X						
The Sound Bus		X		X	X				X	
Apples on a Tree								X		
All About My Name	X	X		X	X			X	X	X

Shoe Box Learning Centers: Alphabet   Scholastic Teaching Resources

Breakfast Words

Children match letters to spell cereal names.

Materials

- shoe box
- box label
- student directions
- scissors
- glue
- empty cereal boxes
  (single serving size; or cereal box templates, page 10)
- alphabet boards (pages 11–12)
- resealable plastic bags

Shoe Box Setup

Cut out the fronts from several different cereal boxes. Copy the alphabet boards. Make letter tiles by cutting apart the letters on each board. Place each set of letter tiles in a resealable bag. Place the cereal box fronts and letter tiles in the shoe box. Glue the label to one end of the box and the student directions to the inside of the lid.

TIP Have children say the name of the cereal. Encourage them to think of other words that start with the same sound. For variations on this activity, substitute other food boxes such as those for noodles, crackers, and cookies. For an extra challenge, children can sort the packages into ABC order by initial letter.

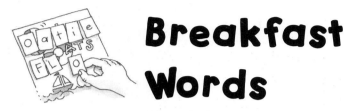

Distinguishing Letter Forms

Breakfast Words

Directions

① Choose a cereal box front.

② Match the alphabet letters to the letters in the cereal name. Place the letters on the box.

③ Choose a new cereal and repeat.

Breakfast Words

Shoe Box Learning Centers: Alphabet   Scholastic Teaching Resources

Alphabet Board

A	B	C	D	E
F	G	H	I	J
K	L	M	N	O
P	Q	R	S	T
U	V	W	X	Y
Z				

Alphabet Board

a	b	c	d	e
f	g	h	i	j
k	l	m	n	o
p	q	r	s	t
u	v	w	x	y
z				

Shoe Box Learning Centers: Alphabet   Scholastic Teaching Resources

Spill the Letters Match-Up

Children play a bean game to practice identifying uppercase and lowercase letters.

Materials

- shoe box
- box label
- student directions
- scissors
- glue
- mini alphabet boards (page 14)
- dried lima beans
- marker
- resealable plastic bag
- plastic cup or shaker

Shoe Box Setup

Copy the alphabet boards onto card stock. Write uppercase letters on one side of the beans and their matching lowercase letters on the other. Make two sets of lima bean letters. Place the beans in the bag. Place the boards, beans, and cup inside the shoe box. Glue the label to one end of the box and the student directions to the inside of the lid.

TIP As a variation, write the letters of the alphabet on adding machine tape (in place of the alphabet boards). Make one for uppercase letters and one for lowercase letters. When children spill the beans, have them match the beans to letters on their tape. Bingo chips or two-colored counters may be substituted for beans.

Differentiating Between Uppercase and Lowercase Letters

Spill the Letters Match-Up

Directions
(for 2 players)

1. One player takes the uppercase alphabet board. The other player takes the lowercase alphabet board.

2. Place five beans in the cup. Take turns following these directions:

   - Shake and spill the beans.
   - Place matching beans on the board (only lowercase letters on a lowercase board, only uppercase letters on an uppercase board).
   - Return unmatched beans to the cup. Add more beans, if needed, to equal five.

3. Play until all the beans are on a board. Trade boards and play again.

Spill the Letters Match-Up

A	B	C	D
E	F	G	H
I	J	K	L
M	N	O	P
Q	R	S	T
U	V	W	X
Y	Z		

Spill the Letters Match-Up

a	b	c	d
e	f	g	h
i	j	k	l
m	n	o	p
q	r	s	t
u	v	w	x
y	z		

Shoe Box Learning Centers: Alphabet   Scholastic Teaching Resources

Conversation-Heart Messages

Children match different fonts of commercially produced letters to those on a handwritten valentine message.

Materials

- shoe box
- box label
- student directions
- scissors
- glue
- heart cutouts (page 16)
- candy conversation hearts
- covered plastic container
- printed material
  (such as magazines, newspapers, and computer printouts)

Shoe Box Setup

Copy the heart templates onto card stock and cut them apart. Place the candy hearts in a covered plastic container. (In place of candy hearts, you can write messages on some of the heart templates—for example, "Hug me" and "Be mine.") Place the hearts, printed material, scissors, and glue in the shoe box. Glue the label to one end of the box and the student directions to the inside of the lid.

TIP As a writing extension, let children create their own conversation hearts by writing or dictating messages.

Identifying Printed Forms of Letters

Conversation-Heart Messages

♡ ♡ ♡

Directions

① Choose a candy heart.

② Find and cut out the first letter. Match it to the letter on the heart. Repeat with each letter on the heart.

③ When you've matched all the letters, glue them in order on a blank heart.

④ Choose a new heart and repeat.

Conversation-Heart Messages

Shoe Box Learning Centers: Alphabet   Scholastic Teaching Resources

Feely-Box Letters

Children try to identify letters, using their sense of touch.

Materials

- shoe box
- box label
- student directions
- scissors
- glue
- piece of dark cloth (the size of the end of the shoe box)
- plastic letters
- record sheets (page 18)

Shoe Box Setup

Cut a hole in one end of the shoe box, big enough to fit a child's hand. Tape the piece of cloth over the hole to make a flap. Block the hole from the inside with a sheet of cardboard while storing the materials. (Remove the cardboard to use the center.) Place the letters and record sheets in the shoe box. Glue the label to one end of the box and the student directions to the inside of the lid.

TIP Include both uppercase and lowercase letters in the box. Encourage children to look for matching uppercase and lowercase letters as they begin to accumulate letters that they've correctly guessed. In addition to plastic letters, you may want to use foam or fuzzy letters to add interesting texture.

Recognizing Letters by Shape

Feely-Box Letters

Directions
(for 2 players)

1 Take all the letters out of the box.

2 One player places a letter back in the shoe box. (The other player's eyes are closed.)

3 The other player puts his or her hand inside the box, feels the letter, and names it. If the player correctly names the letter, he or she colors it in on the record sheet.

4 Players take turns placing letters in the box and guessing them. Play until there are no more letters to guess.

Name _____ Date _____

Feely-Box Letters

A   B   C   D   E   F   G
H   I   J   K   L   M   N
O   P   Q   R   S   T   U
V   W   X   Y   Z

- -

Name _____ Date _____

Feely-Box Letters

A   B   C   D   E   F   G
H   I   J   K   L   M   N
O   P   Q   R   S   T   U
V   W   X   Y   Z

Shoe-Box Learning Centers: Alphabet · Scholastic Teaching Resources

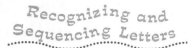

Up and Down the Beanstalk

Children sequence letters of the alphabet as they climb up and down a beanstalk.

Materials

- shoe box
- box label
- student directions
- scissors
- glue
- beanstalks (page 20)
- green crayon
- dried white kidney beans
- permanent marker

Shoe Box Setup

Copy the beanstalks onto card stock and cut them apart. Color them green. Write each letter of the alphabet on a bean. Make two beans for each letter. Place the beanstalks and beans in the shoe box. Glue the label to one end of the box and the student directions to the inside of the lid.

TIP To reinforce letter sequence, have children sing the ABC song together as they put their beans back in the box, starting with A. For a twist, have them go backward, saying the ABCs from Z to A as they return the beans to the box.

Recognizing and Sequencing Letters

Up and Down the Beanstalk

Directions
(for 2 players)

1 Each player takes a beanstalk. One player is Jack. One player is the giant.

2 Each player takes a bean from the box. Players say the letter on their bean. Players place their bean on the matching letter on their beanstalk.

3 Players take turns taking more beans from the box, one bean at a time. Each bean is placed in ABC order on the beanstalk. If a player already has a letter on a bean, the bean goes back in the box.

4 The first player to fill the beanstalk with the ABCs sings the alphabet song in Jack's or the giant's voice.
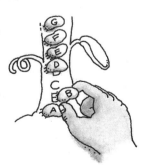

Up and Down
the Beanstalk

Jack

Up and Down
the Beanstalk

Giant

ABC Caterpillar

Children build a caterpillar as they arrange lettered milk caps in alphabetical order.

Materials

- shoe box
- box label
- student directions
- scissors
- glue
- milk caps (or die-cut circles)
- marker
- pipe cleaners
- alphabet boards (pages 11–12)

Shoe Box Setup

To create the caterpillar's head, draw a face on one milk cap and attach pipe cleaner antennae. Label 26 additional milk caps with letters of the alphabet. Make copies of the alphabet boards. Place the milk caps and alphabet boards inside the shoe box. Glue the label to one end of the box and the student directions to the inside of the lid.

TIP To extend the activity, let children work with partners. Once children have placed all the milk caps in alphabetical order, have them continue to strengthen letter recognition as they put the milk caps away. To do this, have one child name a letter. The other child finds it and returns it to the shoe box. Children continue in this way, taking turns naming and finding letters, until all the milk caps are back in the box.

Recognizing Alphabetical Order

ABC Caterpillar

Directions

1 Find the caterpillar's head and place it in front of you.

2 Choose milk caps from the shoe box one at a time. Use the milk caps to build a caterpillar by placing them in alphabetical order. Use the alphabet board to help you.

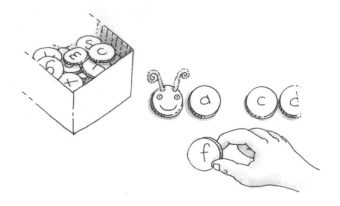

The Mystery of the Missing Letters

This shoe box center turns students into detectives as they solve the mystery of missing letters.

Materials

- shoe box
- box label
- student directions
- scissors
- glue
- alphabet boards (pages 11–12)
- envelopes
- paper (cut to letter-tile size)
- pencils
- magnifier (optional)

Shoe Box Setup

Make multiple copies of the alphabet boards on card stock. Cut apart the letters to make letter tiles. Place each set of letters in an envelope. Remove one letter from each envelope. Place the envelopes, blank letter tiles, pencils, and magnifier in the shoe box. Glue the label to one end of the box and the student directions to the inside of the lid.

TIP For added fun, children can use the magnifier as a prop for "discovering" the missing letters. Include an alphabet board for reference (pages 11–12) to assist children in placing the letters in alphabetical order and determining the missing letter in each envelope.

The Mystery of the Missing Letters

Directions

1. Choose an envelope. Take out the letters.

2. Put the letters in order. Find out which letter is missing.

3. Write the missing letter on a blank letter tile. Put it in the correct place.

4. Choose a new envelope. Repeat steps 1 through 3.

22

Lost and Found

Children sequence letters from a box to identify which are missing, and then find them in the Lost and Found.

Materials

- shoe box
- box label
- student directions
- scissors
- glue
- mini erasers (various shapes and colors)
- permanent marker
- small boxes

Shoe Box Setup

Write each letter of the alphabet on a small eraser (or write on stickers and place them on the erasers). Repeat to make several sets of letters. Remove several different letters from each set and place them in a box labeled "Lost and Found." Place each set of erasers in a small box. Place the boxes and Lost and Found box in the shoe box. Glue the label to one end of the box and the student directions to the inside of the lid.

TIP Introduce this activity by sharing *The Letters Are Lost*, by Lisa Campbell Ernst (Viking, 1996), which invites young readers to find the alphabet blocks that were once together in a box.

Recognizing and Sequencing Letters

Lost and Found

Directions

1. Choose a box.

2. Take out the erasers. Place the erasers in ABC order.

3. Search for the missing letters in the Lost and Found box.

4. Place the letters you find in the missing spaces.

5. Choose a new toy box and repeat.

Match the Mix-Ups

Children practice identifying and matching commonly mixed-up letters.

Materials

- shoe box
- box label
- student directions
- scissors
- glue
- mix-up boards (pages 25–26)
- spinner pattern (page 26)
- pencil
- paper clip
- lowercase letter tiles *b, d, p,* and *q* (two sets)
- uppercase letter tiles *M* and *W* (two sets)

Shoe Box Setup

Copy the mix-up boards and spinner onto card stock. Place the boards, spinner, pencil, paper clip, and letter tiles in the shoe box. Glue the label to one end of the box and the student directions to the inside of the lid. Note: If desired, the letter *q* that appears in the art on page 25 can be modified by simply adding a "tail." Do the same for the spinner on page 26.

TIP Have children create their own pictures that incorporate other commonly confused lowercase and uppercase letters, including *a, g; g, q; g, p; i, j; h, b; r, n; n, m; v, y; F, E; C, G; O, Q; P, R; P, B;* and *V, W.*

Match the Mix-Ups

Directions
(for 2 players)

1 Each player takes a mix-up board and one of each of the following lowercase letters: *m, w, b, d, p,* and *q.*

2 To use the spinner, place the pencil and paper clip in the center. Players take turns spinning the paper clip. They match the letter they land on to one on their mix-up board, then place the same letter tile on the board.

3 The first player to match all the letters wins.

Match the Mix-Ups

Match the Mix-Ups

Match the Mix-Ups

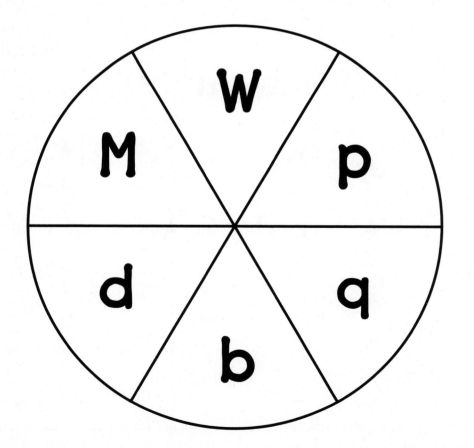

Shoe Box Learning Centers: Alphabet   Scholastic Teaching Resources

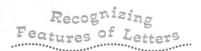
Trace and Race

Children trace letters in segments as they race to be the first to reach *Z*.

Materials

- shoe box
- box label
- student directions
- scissors
- glue
- alphabet boards (pages 11–12)
- crayons
- number cubes

Shoe Box Setup

Make copies of the alphabet boards. Place the alphabet boards, crayons, and number cubes in the shoe box. Glue the label to one end of the box and the student directions to the inside of the lid.

TIP **F**or variations on this game, children can also work from *Z* to *A* or trace over all the letters in their name (or any other specified word).

Recognizing Features of Letters

Trace and Race

Directions
(for 2 or more players)

(1) Each player takes an alphabet board and a crayon.

(2) Players take turns rolling the number cube and tracing over that number of parts on a letter. Players begin with the letter *A*. Each straight or curved section counts as one part. An *A* is 3 parts. A *B* is 3 parts. A *C* is 1 part. You can trace more than one letter in one turn.

Examples:
If you roll a 6, you can trace over *A* (3 parts) and *B* (3 parts).

If you roll a 4, you can trace over *A* and 1 part of *B*.

(3) The first player to trace over *Z* wins the game.

Letter Collages

Children create crayon-rubbing collages with textured letters.

Materials

- shoe box
- box label
- student directions
- scissors
- glue
- sandpaper
- corrugated cardboard
- index cards
- colored glue
- crayons
- paper

Shoe Box Setup

To make textured letters, cut out letter shapes from sandpaper and corrugated cardboard. Make a third set by writing the letters of the alphabet on index cards and tracing them with colored glue; let dry. Place the three sets of textured letters, crayons, and paper in the shoe box. Glue the label to one end of the box and the student directions to the inside of the lid.

TIP Children can also use the textured letters to make letter collages according to specified criteria. Make copies of the prompts on page 29. Cut out the prompts and glue each to a sheet of paper to make master copies. Make copies of each, and add them to the shoe box. Have children find and make rubbings of letters that fit each criterion (such as "Letters With Only Straight Lines") and glue the appropriate label to the paper.

Exploring Features of Letters

Letter Collages

Directions

1. Choose a letter. Place it under your paper.

2. Use the crayons to make a rubbing of your letter.

3. Continue with other letters to create a collage. Say the letters you make.

Letter Collage Prompts

Letters With
Only Straight Lines

Letters With Only
Curved Lines

Letters With Straight
and Curved Lines

Letters in
My Name

Letters I Know

Letters Not
in My Name

Snowy Day Letters

Children practice forming letters by writing them in snow.

Materials

- shoe box
- box label
- student directions
- scissors
- glue
- paint (any color but white)
- snowflake patterns (page 31)
- record sheets (page 32)
- powdered soap flakes
- small sticks
- pencils

Shoe Box Setup

Paint the inside bottom of the shoe box. Make copies of the snowflake patterns and write a different letter of the alphabet on each. Make copies of the record sheets and cut apart. Sprinkle the soap flake snow in the box to cover the bottom. Place the snowflake letters, record sheets, sticks, and pencils in the shoe box. Glue the label to one end of the box and the student directions to the inside of the lid.

TIP If powdered soap flakes are unavailable, substitute fake snow or salt. You may want to introduce this activity by reading aloud *The Snowy Day*, by Ezra Jack Keats (Viking Press, 1962), a Caldecott Medal classic about a young boy exploring freshly fallen snow.

Forming Letters

Snowy Day Letters

Directions

(1) Choose a snowflake. Read the letter.

(2) Use the stick to write the letter in the snow.

(3) Write the letter on your record sheet.

(4) Choose a new snowflake and repeat.

Snowy Day Letters

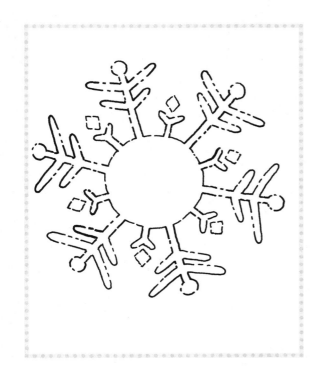

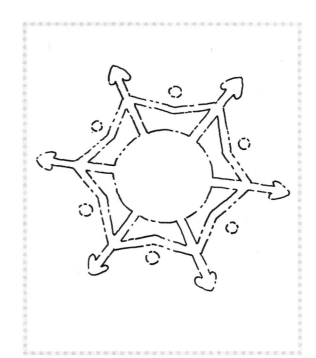

Name _____ Date _____

Snowy Day Letters

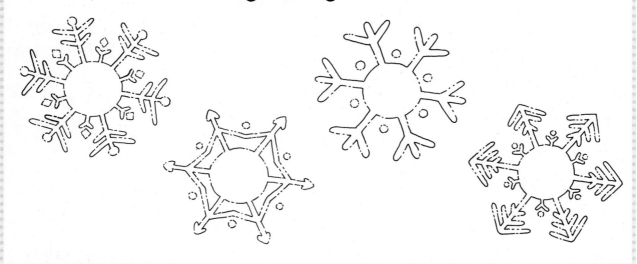

- -

Name _____ Date _____

Snowy Day Letters

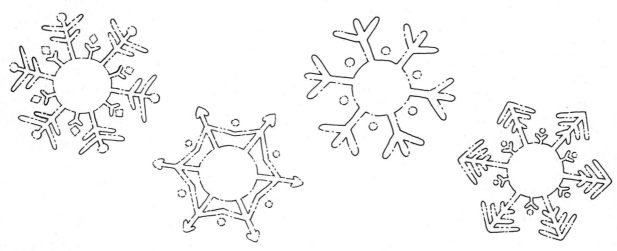

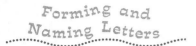

Airplane ABCs

Children use white crayon and blue paint to make "airplane writing" letters appear in the sky.

Materials

- shoe box
- box label
- student directions
- scissors
- glue
- paper airplanes
- white crayons
- string
- white drawing paper
- blue paint
- paintbrushes

Shoe Box Setup

Use string to attach a white crayon to each paper airplane. (Tie one end of the string around the crayon and tape the other end to the back of the airplane.) Place the airplanes and crayons, drawing paper, paint, and paintbrushes in the shoe box. Glue the label to one end of the box and the student directions to the inside of the lid.

TIP Children can personalize their airplane-writing pictures by adding details. As a variation, children can also do this activity with the letters in their name. Have wipes handy for easy cleanup.

Forming and Naming Letters

Airplane ABCs

Directions

(1) Using the white crayon (attached to the airplane), write the letters of the alphabet on a sheet of paper.

(2) Paint over the letters with blue paint.

(3) Look at the letters in the sky! Say each letter in order.

(4) Take the string and crayon off the airplane. Glue the airplane to the picture.

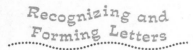
Tweet-Tweet Letter Treats

Children create an alphabet feast for birds by forming yarn worms into letters.

Materials

- shoe box
- box label
- student directions
- scissors
- glue
- letter treats templates (page 35)
- yarn (several colors)
- resealable plastic bag

Shoe Box Setup

Make copies of the letter treats templates and cut apart. Write a different letter of the alphabet on each nest. Cut yarn into "worms" (ranging from one to six inches each). Place the yarn in the bag. Place the letter treats templates, yarn, and glue in the shoe box. Glue the label to one end of the box and the student directions to the inside of the lid.

TIP For reusable nests and removable worms, substitute pipe cleaners or Wikki Stix for yarn. Children can also practice sequencing skills by arranging their nests in ABC order.

Tweet-Tweet Letter Treats

Directions

1 Choose a bird. Read the letter on its nest.

2 Make food for the bird: Use the yarn worms to form that letter. Glue the letter in place.

3 Choose a new bird and repeat.

Tweet-Tweet Letter Treats
Name Rita Date May 3

Name _____

Date _____

Tweet-Tweet Letter Treats

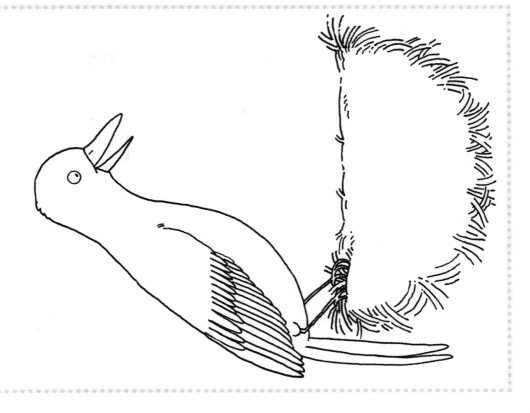

Name _____

Date _____

Tweet-Tweet Letter Treats

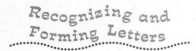

Rainy Day Writing

Children form letters with "raindrops."

Materials

- shoe box
- box label
- student directions
- scissors
- glue
- markers
- resealable plastic bag
- blank transparencies
- eyedroppers
- small plastic cups
- paper towels

Shoe Box Setup

Write each letter of the alphabet (or those letters that you want children to practice forming) on a large (five to six inches square) sheet of white card stock. Use brightly colored markers for visual appeal. Store the cards in a resealable bag. Place the bag, transparencies, eyedroppers, cups, and paper towels in the shoe box. Glue the label to one end of the box and the student directions to the inside of the lid.

TIP Children love experimenting with colors. Add this option by including food coloring in the shoe box. Invite children to add a drop or two to the water in their cup.

Recognizing and Forming Letters

Rainy Day Writing

Directions

1. Choose a letter card. Say the letter name.
2. Put water in a cup.
3. Place a plastic sheet over the letter.
4. Use the eyedropper to make the letter with drops of water.
5. Wipe off the water. Choose a new letter and repeat.

Cups of Cocoa

Children explore features of letters as they outline them with mini marshmallows.

Materials

- shoe box
- box label
- student directions
- scissors
- glue
- cocoa cup patterns (page 38)
- mini marshmallows

Shoe Box Setup

Copy the cups onto card stock and cut them apart. Make one for each letter you want to include. Write a letter on each cup, and decorate the cup if desired. Place the cups and marshmallows in the shoe box. Glue the label to one end of the box and the student directions to the inside of the lid.

TIP Have children examine the letters they form. Which have straight lines? Curved? Do any of them look like alike (for example, *b* and *d*)? Invite children to explain similarities and differences among letters.

Recognizing and Forming Letters

Cups of Cocoa

Directions

1. Choose a cup. Say the letter on the cup.

2. Use marshmallows to make the letter.

3. Choose a new cup and repeat.

Cups of Cocoa

ABC Snapshots

Children find and trace the shape of letters found in pictures of objects.

Materials

- shoe box
- box label
- student directions
- scissors
- glue
- small photo album with plastic sleeves (for 4- by 6-inch photos)
- pictures from magazines (showing objects that reflect the shape of letters—for example, an *O* in a clock, an *E, F,* and *T* in a window frame, and an *L* in a fence)
- stick-on labels (such as those for file folders)
- wipe-off markers
- socks

Shoe Box Setup

Cut pictures to fit the photo album sleeves. Place each in a sleeve. Place a label at the bottom of each page. Write a letter that children can look for in the picture. Fill the photo album with pictures. Place the photo album, markers, and socks in the shoe box. Glue the label to one end of the box and the student directions to the inside of the lid.

TIP Let children further explore this concept by reading Stephen Johnson's Caldecott Medal winner *Alphabet City* (Puffin, 1999). Can they find letter shapes in any objects in the classroom? Children can draw these letter pictures on paper to make a class book.

Recognizing and Forming Letters

ABC Snapshots

Directions

1. Open the photo album. Find and name the letter in the first picture.

2. Trace over the letter using the marker.

3. Use the sock to wipe off the letter.

4. Go to the next picture and repeat.

Alphabet Soup

Children discover features of letter shapes (straight and curved lines) by using pasta shapes to make alphabet soup.

Materials

- shoe box
- box label
- student directions
- scissors
- glue
- alphabet boards (pages 11–12)
- soup bowl patterns (page 41)
- uncooked linguini and elbow macaroni

Shoe Box Setup

Copy the alphabet boards onto card stock. Cut apart the letters to make letter tiles. Make card-stock copies of the soup bowls. Place the letter tiles, soup bowls, and pasta in the shoe box. Glue the label to one end of the box and the student directions to the inside of the lid.

TIP To further reinforce alphabet skills, have children use their fingers to trace each letter they make and say the corresponding name and sound. Children can also arrange the bowls they create in alphabetical order. Copy another set of alphabet boards and include them in the shoe box as an alphabet chart reference.

Discriminating Similarities and Differences in Letters

Alphabet Soup

Directions

1 Choose a letter tile. Say the letter name.

2 Use the noodles to form the letter. You can break straight noodles into pieces.

3 Glue the letter on the soup bowl.

4 Choose a new letter tile and repeat.

Name _____ Date _____

Alphabet Soup

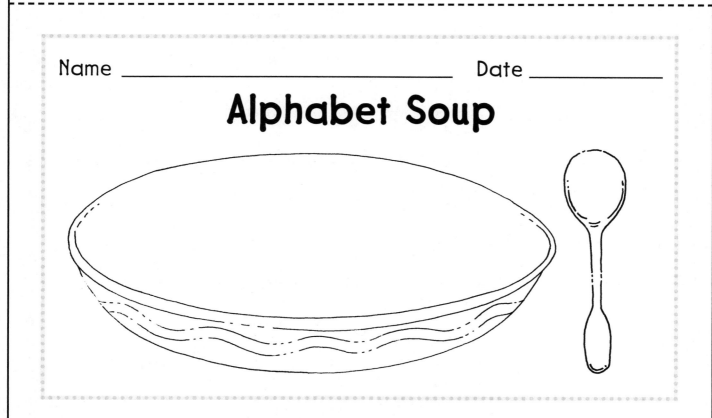

Name _____ Date _____

Alphabet Soup

Cloudy Day ABCs

**Children discover features of letter
shapes (straight and curved lines) by
making cotton ball clouds.**

Materials

- shoe box
- box label
- student directions
- scissors
- glue
- index cards
- cotton balls
- blue paper

Shoe Box Setup

Make letter cards by writing each
letter of the alphabet on an index
card. Place the cards, cotton balls, paper,
and glue in the shoe box. Glue the label
to one end of the box and the student
directions to the inside of the lid.

TIP **T**o further reinforce alphabet
skills, have children use
their fingers to trace each letter
they make and say the corresponding
letter name and sound. Children can also
use individual sheets of paper for each
letter they create (cut the paper into
smaller pieces) and arrange the letters in
alphabetical order. Copy the alphabet
boards on pages 11–12 and include them
in the shoe box as reference.

Discriminating Similarities and
Differences in Letter Shapes

Cloudy Day ABCs

Directions

① Choose a letter card. Say the letter
name.

② Use cotton balls to make the letter on
a sheet of paper. Glue the cotton
balls on the paper.

③ Choose a new letter card and
repeat.

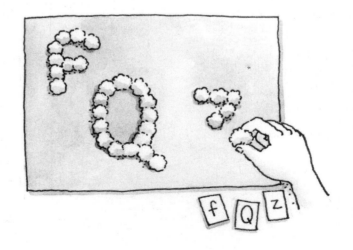

Handmade Names

Children use finger spelling to spell classmates' names.

Materials

- shoe box
- box label
- student directions
- scissors
- glue
- finger-spelling alphabet cards (pages 44–46)
- name-picture cards

Shoe Box Setup

Copy the finger-spelling alphabet cards onto card stock and cut them apart. Make multiple sets. (Some names will require more than one of the same letter.) Write each student's name on a sentence strip. Glue students' pictures next to their name. Place the alphabet and name cards in the shoe box. Glue the label to one end of the box and the student directions to the inside of the lid.

TIP Introduce this activity by sharing *The Handmade Alphabet*, by Laura Rankin (Dial, 1991), a Reading Rainbow book that shows finger spellings along with the written alphabet and corresponding pictures.

Forming Letters With the Finger-Spelling Alphabet

Handmade Names

Directions

(1) Choose a name card.

(2) Find the finger-spelling alphabet cards that match the letters on the name card. Place the finger-spelling alphabet cards in order on the name card.

(3) Use your fingers to spell each letter of your name.

(4) Choose a new card and repeat.

J a c k

Handmade Names

Aa	Bb	Cc

Dd	Ee	Ff

Gg	Hh	Ii

Handmade Names

Jj

Kk

Ll

Mm

Nn

Oo

Pp

Qq

Rr

Handmade Names

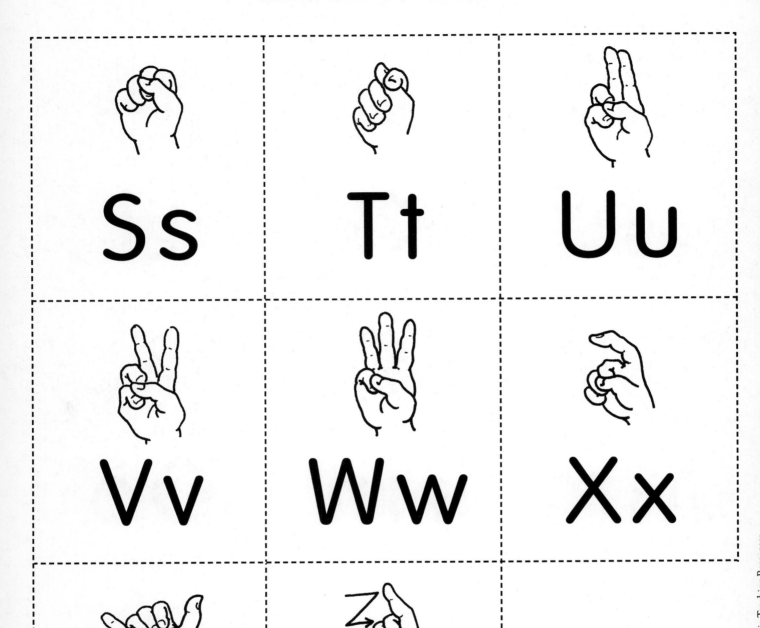

S s   T t   U u

V v   W w   X x

Y y   Z z

Vroom! Vroom!

Children drive cars to practice blending letter sounds to make words.

Materials

- shoe box
- box label
- student directions
- scissors
- glue
- word cards (page 48)
- miniature toy cars

Shoe Box Setup

Copy and cut apart the word cards. Make additional word cards as desired. (See Tip, below.) Place the word cards and cars in the shoe box. Glue the label to one end of the box and the student directions to the inside of the lid.

TIP When introducing this activity, start with simple CVC words that represent common sound-spelling relationships. In addition to the word cards on page 48, you might make the following word cards for this center: *bat, map, pig, van, pen, gum, cup, mop, log, six,* and *fox.* Include the word and picture (use sticker pictures from old workbooks) on one side and the word only on the other side to offer children two levels of difficulty.

Blending Letter Sounds

Vroom! Vroom!

Directions

① Choose a word card.

② Choose a car. Drive the car over the letters, one at a time. Say the sound of each letter. Say the word the letters make.

③ Choose a new card and repeat.

Vroom! Vroom!

dog

sun

bed

box

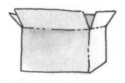

ball

cat

B Is for Butterfly

Children create pictures from letter shapes to make connections between letters, sounds, and words.

Materials

- shoe box
- box label
- student directions
- scissors
- glue
- self-stick labels (such as those for name tags)
- resealable plastic bags
- drawing paper
- crayons

Shoe Box Setup

Make letter stickers by writing each letter of the alphabet on a label. Make several sets of letters. Place each set of stickers in a resealable bag. Place the stickers, paper, and crayons in the shoe box. Glue the label to one end of the box and the student directions to the inside of the lid.

TIP **U**se children's pictures to make an inventive alphabet frieze for the classroom. Try to include at least one picture from every child. Use the picture letters to review the alphabet. Together, say the name of the letter, the name of the picture, and the sound the letter makes. Children who are ready to write words to go with their pictures can write and complete the following sentence frame: _____ is for _____. Have students glue the sentence frame to their pictures.

Connecting Letters, Sounds, and Words

B Is for Butterfly

B is for "Butterfly"

Directions

1. Choose a letter.

2. Stick the letter to a sheet of paper. Think of something that starts with this letter. Draw a picture using the letter.

3. Choose a new letter and repeat.

B is for "Butterfly"   O is for "Ouch"

On Alphabet Street

Children create an alphabet book of beginning sounds.

Materials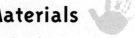

- shoe box
- box label
- student directions
- scissors
- glue
- house pattern (page 51)
- pictures from old workbooks or worksheets

Shoe Box Setup

Make 26 copies of the house pattern. Write a different letter of the alphabet on the door of each house. Put the pages in alphabetical order, add a cover, and staple to bind. (Repeat to make more than one book, if desired.) Gather pictures from old workbooks or worksheets. Place the book, pictures, and glue in the shoe box. Glue the label to one end of the box and the student directions to the inside of the lid.

TIP In addition to pictures, student photos, stickers, and rubber stamps are fun to use in these books. To make a lift-the-flap book, cut around three sides of each window to create flaps. Glue the edges of each book page to a sheet of paper (use a color other than white for contrast). Put the pages in order and staple to bind. Have children glue their pictures under the window flaps. For writing practice, have them write the corresponding letter on the outside of each window.

Recognizing Beginning Letter-Sound Relationships

On Alphabet Street

Directions

1. Take one copy of the book "On Alphabet Street."

2. Choose a picture. Say the name of the picture. Listen for the beginning sound.

3. In the book, find the house with the letter that matches the sound. Paste the picture in a window.

4. Choose a new picture and repeat.

On Alphabet Street

Buried Treasure

Children dig for treasures and sort what they find by beginning letters.

Materials

- shoe box
- box label
- student directions
- scissors
- glue
- treasure chest patterns (page 53)
- print materials (such as magazines)
- treasures (such as play coins, jewels, buttons, stones, and beads)
- packing peanuts
- toy shovels

Shoe Box Setup

Make copies of the treasure chests and cut them apart. Cut out letters of the alphabet from magazines or other print materials. Glue a letter to each treasure to match the beginning sound of its name. Write a letter on each treasure chest to coordinate with the treasures you include. Fill the shoe box partway with packing peanuts. Bury the treasures in the packing peanuts. Place the treasure chests and shovels in the shoe box. Glue the label to one end of the box and the student directions to the inside of the lid.

TIP Make extra copies of the treasure chests to use as record sheets. Add spaces for children to write their name and the date. Have children complete a record sheet for each treasure chest they place treasures in, writing the letter on the record sheet and drawing pictures to show the treasures they found.

Recognizing Letter-Sound Relationships

Buried Treasure

Directions

1. Use a shovel to dig for treasure.

2. Say the name of each treasure.

3. Sort your treasures by beginning letter into the treasure chests.

Buried Treasure

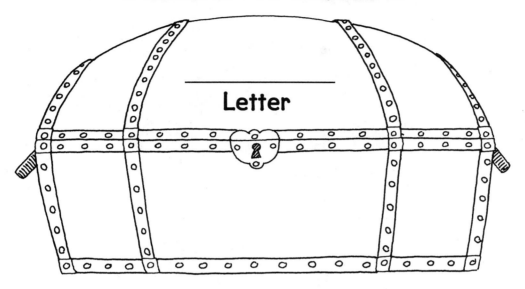

_____
Letter

Buried Treasure

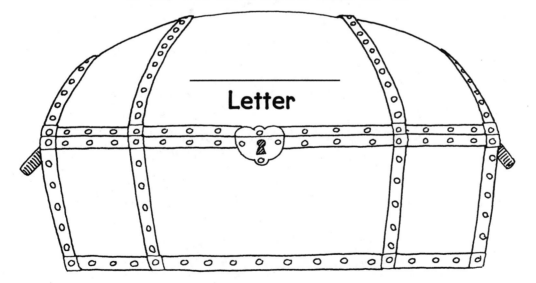

_____
Letter

It's a Parade!

Children use beginning sounds to line up colorful animals in parade formation.

Materials

- shoe box
- box label
- student directions
- scissors
- glue
- parade mats (page 55)
- parade markers (page 56)
- small plastic animals
- cardboard

Shoe Box Setup

Make multiple copies of the parade mat, cut apart the strips, and tape A to B. Make multiple copies of the parade markers and cut them apart. Label each parade marker with a letter. Collect several dozen small plastic animals with beginning letters that represent different letters of the alphabet, including those on the parade markers. (Look for assortment packs at toy stores or online sources.) Cut a hole sized to fit a child's hand in one end of the shoe box. Block the hole temporarily with a piece of cardboard while storing the materials. Place the parade mats, parade markers, and animals in the shoe box. Glue the label to one end of the box and the student directions to the inside of the lid.

TIP At the end of the game, challenge children to put their parade lineup in alphabetical order. For an extra challenge, invite them to work together to collectively line up their parade animals in alphabetical order.

Recognizing Letter Sounds

It's a Parade!

Directions
(for 2 or more players)

① Each player chooses six parade markers and a parade mat. Players line up their markers on the parade mat in any order.

② Choose one animal and set it outside the box. This is the discard pile. Leave the other animals in the box and replace the lid.

③ Take turns following these directions:
- Take an animal (the animal outside the box or one inside the box).
- If the animal's name begins with a letter that is part of your parade, place it on that marker. If not, place it in the discard pile.

④ Play until all parade markers are filled in.

It's a Parade!

It's a Parade!

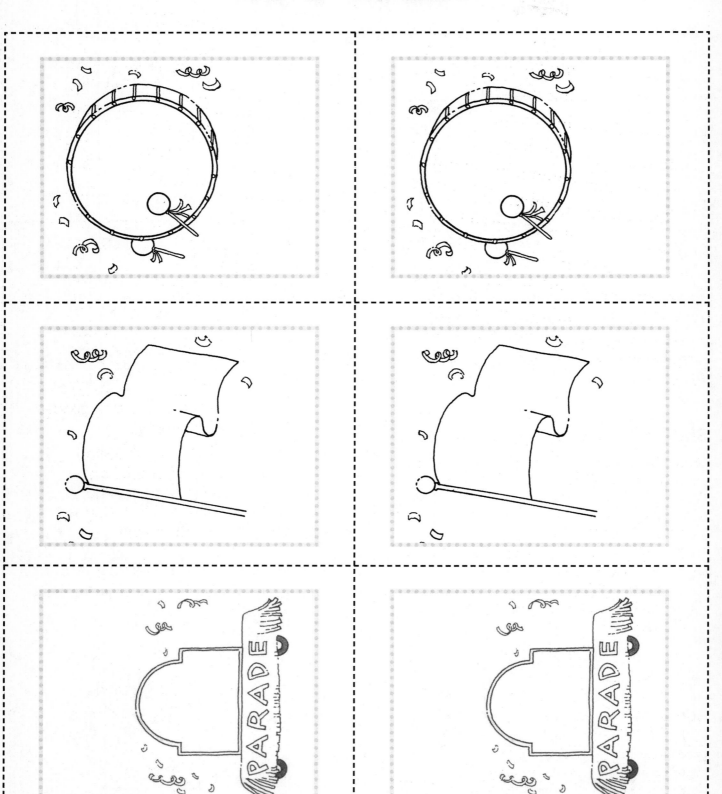

Check It Out!

Children identify beginning letter sounds in the names of favorite book characters as they "check out" favorite books.

Materials

- shoe box
- box label
- student directions
- scissors
- glue
- book patterns (page 58)
- bookshelf patterns (page 59)
- pictures of book characters
- mini canvas bags (available at craft stores or online sources)
- alphabet letters (plastic, foam, or tile)

Shoe Box Setup

Copy the book and bookshelf patterns onto card stock. Collect pictures of book characters or recognizable covers from book club order forms, catalogs, or ads. Glue one picture onto each book and laminate. Place the books, bookshelves, book bags, and alphabet letters in the shoe box. Glue the label to one end of the box and the student directions to the inside of the lid.

TIP Involve children in creating the books by inviting them to cut out pictures of their favorite characters from extra book club flyers. As children cut out the pictures, encourage discussion about the characters: What words describe each character? What do students like most about the characters? Do any of the characters have something in common?

Recognizing Letter Sounds

Check It Out!

Directions

(1) Check out six library "books" and place them in your book bag.

(2) Pull out one book at a time and place it on a bookshelf. Name the character and place its beginning letter sound on top of the book.

(3) When the bookshelf is full, place the books in alphabetical order.

(4) Return the books to the library (the shoe box). Choose six more.

Check It Out!

Check It Out!

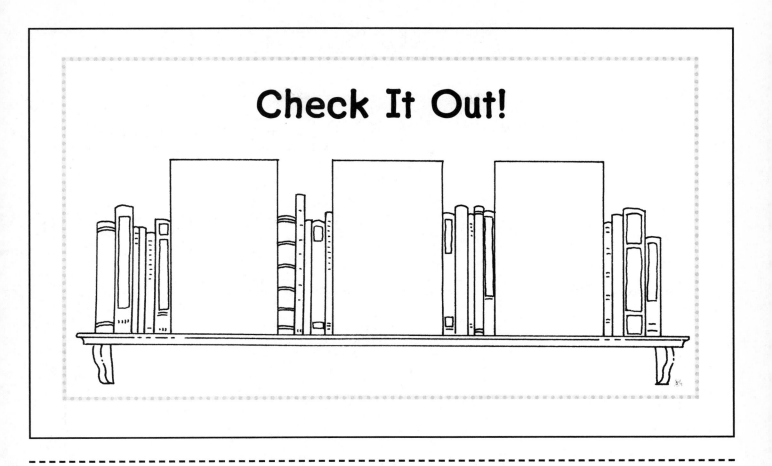

Check It Out!

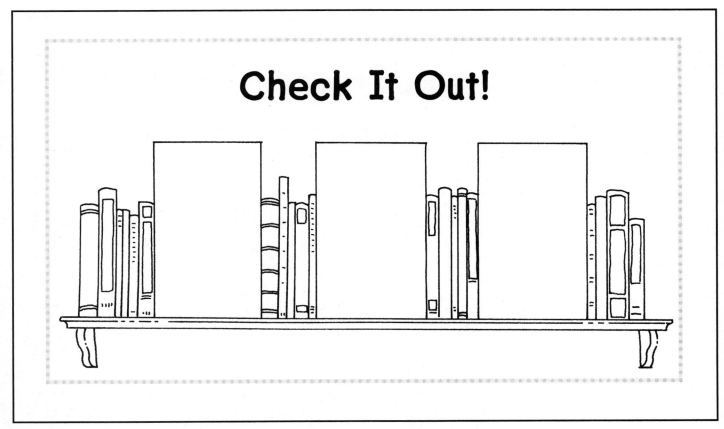

Musical Letters

Children name strings of sounds that form a musical pattern.

Materials

- shoe box
- box label
- student directions
- scissors
- glue
- xylophone
- removable dot stickers
- sound strips (page 61)
- alphabet letters (letter tiles or plastic letters; multiples of each letter)

Shoe Box Setup

Use dot stickers to label the keys of the xylophone with different letters of the alphabet. Copy the sound strips onto card stock. Using the letters on the xylophone, write a letter pattern (for example, *aaeegg*) inside the notes on each strip. Cut apart the strips. Place the sound strips and alphabet letters in the shoe box. Place the xylophone at the center where children will be doing this activity. Glue the label to one end of the box and the student directions to the inside of the lid.

TIP Children may want to try playing the letter patterns on other musical instruments such as a recorder or a keyboard.

Recognizing Letter Sounds

Musical Letters

Directions

(1) Choose a sound strip. Find those letters on the xylophone.

(2) Play the letter pattern on the xylophone. Say the sound of each letter.

(3) Choose a new sound strip and repeat.

(4) Use the alphabet letters to create your own letter patterns.

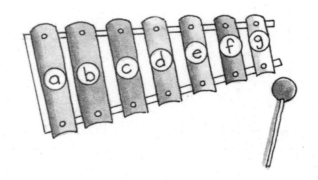

Musical Letters

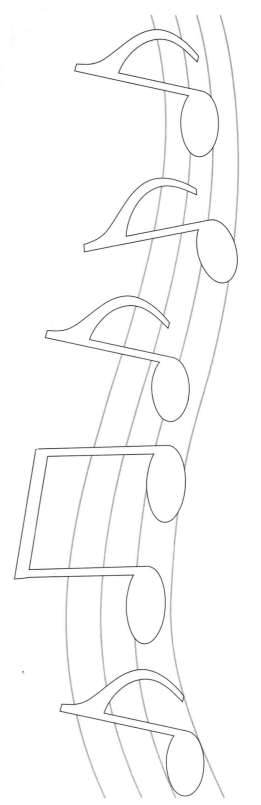

Musical Letters

The Sound Bus

Children identify the position of a letter sound in a word.

Materials

- shoe box
- box label
- student directions
- scissors
- glue
- picture cards (pages 63–65)
- sound bus pattern (page 66)
- small toy people

Shoe Box Setup

Copy the picture cards onto card stock and cut them apart. Make multiple copies of the sound bus. Place the picture cards, buses, and toy people in the shoe box. Glue the label to one end of the box and the student directions to the inside of the lid.

TIP Bingo chips can be substituted for the small plastic figures that are "riding" the sound bus. For a variation and a challenge, place each picture card in an envelope with letter cards that represent each phoneme in the word. (Use pictures for words with three phonemes to fit the three sections of the bus template.) For example, to go with a picture of a cat, include the letters *c*, *a*, and *t*. For a fish, include the letters *f*, *i*, and *sh*. Have children place the letter cards in order on the bus to form the word.

Recognizing Phonemes

The Sound Bus

Directions

(1) Take a sound bus and some toy people.

(2) Choose a picture card. Say the word that names the picture.

(3) Read the letter on the card. Say the sound it makes. Place a person on the bus in the spot where you hear that sound.

(4) Choose a new card and repeat. Line up your pictures in order beneath the bus.

The Sound Bus (Beginning Sounds)

b	d	f	g
h	l	m	n
p	s	t	v

Shoe Box Learning Centers: Alphabet   Scholastic Teaching Resources

The Sound Bus (Middle Sounds)

b	k	d	g
r	l	p	t
n	f	m	w

Shoe Box Learning Centers: Alphabet   Scholastic Teaching Resources

The Sound Bus (Ending Sounds)

b	d	g	k

l	m	n	p

r	s	t	k

The Sound Bus

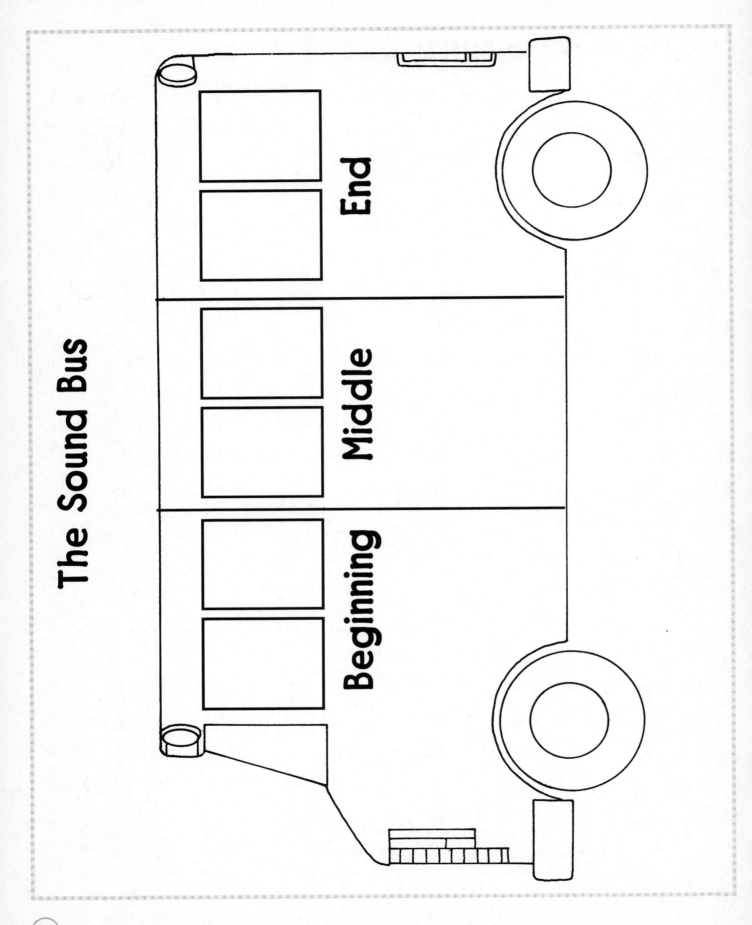

End

Middle

Beginning

Hearing Word Parts

Apples on a Tree

Children fill a tree with apples as they segment words by the number of sounds they contain.

Materials

- shoe box
- box label
- student directions
- scissors
- glue
- apple tree pattern (page 68)
- picture cards (page 69)
- apple patterns (page 70; or red bingo chips)

Shoe Box Setup

Make several copies of the apple tree pattern and laminate. Copy the picture cards and apple patterns onto card stock and cut apart. Place the apple trees, picture cards, and apple patterns in the shoe box. Glue the label to one end of the box and the student directions to the inside of the lid.

TIP Make this center self-checking by writing the number of sounds on the back of each picture card. For a challenge, children can tell the letter that makes the initial sound (or each of the sounds they hear).

Hearing Word Parts

Apples on a Tree

Directions

1. Take an apple tree.

2. Choose a picture card. Say the word that names the picture.

3. Place an apple on the tree for each sound you hear in the word.

4. Choose a new card and repeat. Play until your tree is full of apples.

la-dy-bug... one, two, three

67

Apples on a Tree

Apples on a Tree

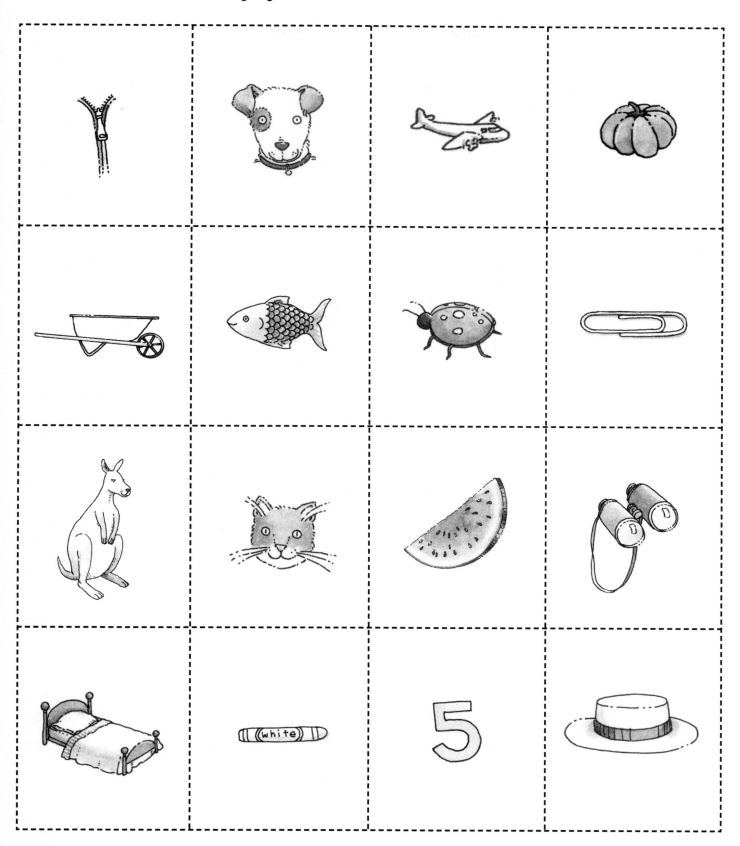

Apples on a Tree

All About My Name

Reusable sorting mats invite children to practice letter recognition and sound-spelling relationships beginning with the words they know best—their names!

Materials

- shoe box
- box label
- student directions
- scissors
- glue
- sorting mats (pages 72–76)
- old workbooks and magazines
- index cards
- alphabet boards (pages 11–12)
- resealable plastic bags
- wet-erase markers
- paper towels

Shoe Box Setup

Make multiple copies of the sorting mats and laminate them. Cut out words and pictures from old workbooks and magazines and glue each to an index card. Store the word and picture cards in a bag. Glue copies of the alphabet boards to tagboard. Cut apart the letters and place each set in a bag (or use tiles or plastic letters). Place the sorting mats, word and picture cards, letters, markers, and paper towels in the shoe box. Glue the label to one end of the box and the student directions to the inside of the lid.

TIP Children can complete these open-ended alphabet mats more than once. When they're ready, they may also create their own word and picture cards to complete the mats.

Recognizing Letters and Sound-Spelling Relationships

All About My Name

Directions
(for 2 players)

1. Choose an alphabet sorting mat.

2. Use the marker to write your name.

3. Use the letters, word cards, or picture cards to complete the mat.

4. Wipe off your name. Try another mat.

All About My Name

My Name _____

Letters in My Name	Letters Not in My Name

All About My Name

My Name _____

Has Fewer Letters Than My Name	Has the Same Number of Letters in My Name	Has More Letters Than My Name

All About My Name

My Name _____

Begins With the Same Sound as My Name	Begins With a Different Sound Than My Name

All About My Name

My Name _____

Ends With the Same Sound as My Name	Ends With a Different Sound Than My Name

All About My Name

My Name _____

Clap and count the sounds in your name.
Sort the word cards or picture cards.

Has Fewer Sounds Than My Name	Has More Sounds Than My Name

More Easy-to-Make Shoe Box Learning Centers

Restock your shoe box centers periodically with fresh activities to keep student interest strong. Following are ideas for making more shoe box centers that reinforce alphabet skills. For each, use the reproducible templates (right) to make a label and write student directions. Glue the label to the outside of the box and the student directions to the inside of the lid.

Letter Sort

Children practice letter recognition with a sorting activity that introduces them to the many different looks one letter can have.

Make letter tiles by cutting letters with different types of fonts from magazines, newspapers, and old greeting cards (or print some from the computer). Paste the letters on card stock and cut them out in small squares. Make copies of the alphabet boards (pages 11–12). Stock a shoe box with the letter tiles, alphabet boards, and glue. Have students sort the letters on the alphabet boards to practice letter recognition.

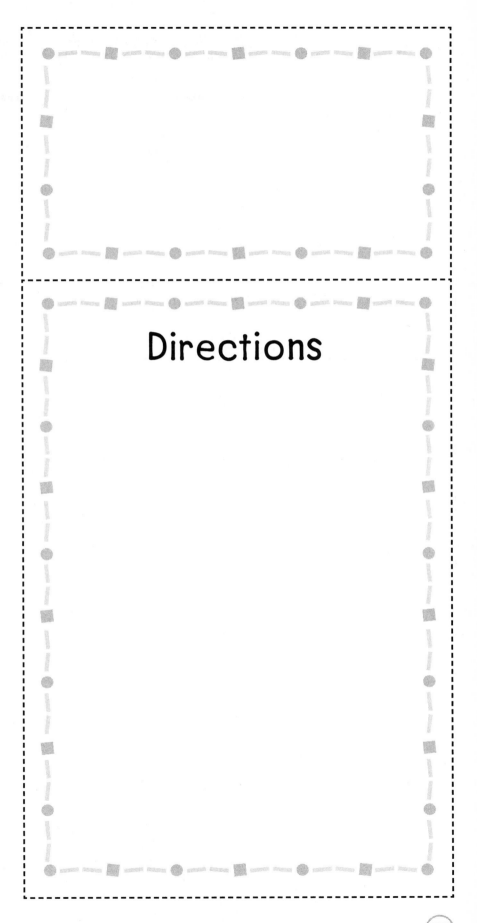

Directions

Alphabet Puzzles

Children use their knowledge of the alphabet letter sequence to put puzzles together.

- Using card stock, make copies of the alphabet boards (pages 11–12). Cut some of the boards apart along the lines to make different-shaped puzzle pieces.

- Place each puzzle in a separate resealable bag. Place the puzzles and intact alphabet boards in the shoe box.

- Have students choose an alphabet board puzzle and put the board back together using what they know about the alphabet.

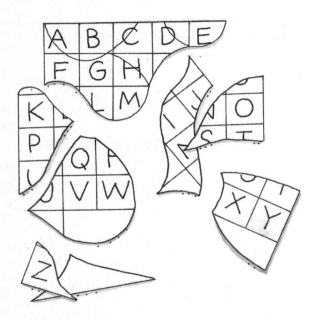

In the Bag

After teaching a letter and its sound, set up a shoe box center to reinforce the skill.

Write the target letter on a paper lunch bag. Place the bag in the box, along with a collection of small toys and other objects. Have children place toys in the bag that they think start with the target letter. Children can create record sheets by drawing pictures of the objects they place in the bag.

Letter Hunt

Reinforce letter recognition with an activity that challenges children to search for and highlight letters found in printed matter.

- Using card stock, make multiple copies of the alphabet boards (pages 11–12) and cut apart each letter.

- Stock the shoe box with the letters, printed material (such as advertising flyers, menus, song lyrics, and extra worksheets), and highlighting markers.

- Have children select a letter and sheet of text and highlight the letter each time they see it on the paper.

- To extend the activity, have children say the name of the letter each time they highlight it. Children can also count the number of times they highlight each letter.

Scrambled Eggs

Children reassemble eggs as they match uppercase and lowercase letters.

- Write an uppercase letter on one half of a plastic egg and a matching lowercase letter on the other. Repeat for each letter of the alphabet. (To discourage matching by color instead of letters, use eggs of one color or mix up the halves to create two-color eggs.)

- Take apart the eggs. Label egg carton cups with letters A to Z. Place the eggs and egg cartons in the shoe box.

- Have children put the eggs together by matching uppercase and lowercase letters and then place the eggs in the cartons in ABC order.

- To provide additional practice recognizing letters, cut paper into egg shapes. Write a letter on each. Have children not only match the egg halves but place the matching paper egg inside.

Adding Machine Tape Letters

Children make mini alphabet friezes while having some fun with rubber stamps.

Stock a shoe box with long pieces of adding machine tape and rubber alphabet stamps. Let children stamp out the letters of the alphabet in order. Provide copies of the alphabet boards (pages 11–12) for reference if desired.

Take-Out Letters

With this center, children match objects to letters to reinforce sound-spelling relationships.

- Write target letters on clean take-out containers (available in craft stores). Stock a shoe box with the containers, grocery store flyers and other sources of food pictures (such as cooking magazines), and scissors.

- Have children cut out pictures of foods that start with the target letters and place them in the corresponding containers.

Magnet Match

Children sort magnetic picture and letter cards to develop letter recognition skills.

- Cut out pictures of recognizable things—for example, dog, cat, airplane, balloon, tractor, car, cake, frog, flower, hot dog, ring, pizza, snowflake, truck, and zebra. Glue each picture to tagboard cut to size and back with a magnetic strip.

- Place the picture cards, magnetic letters (multiple sets), and a mini magnetic board in a shoe box.

- Have children choose a picture card, say the name, and find the matching initial letter, then place the picture and letter pair on the board. Repeat with remaining pictures and letters.

Squishy Letters

This multisensory activity lets children practice letter recognition and formation.

- Fill resealable plastic bags half full with hair gel. Squeeze out excess air and seal. (Use tape to provide a more secure seal.)

- Print each uppercase and lowercase letter of the alphabet on a card. (Make the letters big.)

- Place the cards and bags in a shoe box.

- Have children place a letter card under a bag and trace over it with their finger or the eraser of a pencil as they say the name (and/or sound) of the letter.

Twist-and-Bend Letters

Provide practice with letter recognition, sequence, and formation with this tactile approach.

- Write each letter of the alphabet on an index card. Stock a shoe box with the letter cards and pipe cleaners or Wikki Stix.

- Have children choose a letter card and use a pipe cleaner or Wikki Stix to form the letter. They can place their twist-and-bend letters in ABC order as they make and say them.

Sound Train

This train helps children develop awareness of the different sounds that make up words.

- Stock a shoe box with picture cards. (Cut pictures from magazines and glue them to index cards.)

- Have children choose a picture, say the word for the picture, and count the number of sounds in the word.

- To make a sound train, invite children to look for other pictures with words that have the same number of sounds and place them end to end to form a "train."

- To make a new train, children choose a word with a different number of sounds and repeat.

- To make this center self-checking, write the number of sounds on the back of the picture cards.

Polka-Dot Letters

Reinforce letter formation with a center that invites children to stamp the shape of each letter.

- Stock a shoe box with bingo markers and multiple sets of alphabet letter cards (write each letter on an index card).

- Have children choose a letter card and use the stamper to stamp dots onto the letter shape.

- Have them repeat the activity with a new card and place letters in ABC order as they go. Include wet wipes in the shoe box for easy cleanup.

Letter Crowns

Celebrate children's success by making sparkly crowns that showcase each letter they learn.

- Stock a shoe box with the following materials: strips of tagboard sized to fit children's heads, a stapler or tape, glitter glue, colored paper, jewels, scissors, and print materials (for cutting out letters).

- Help children form the tagboard strips into crowns.

- To decorate the crowns, have children cut out examples of a target letter from print material (flyers, magazines, and so on) and glue them around the outside of the crown. They can use glitter and other art materials to add finishing touches.